HAL•LEONARD

EASY INSTRUMENTAL PLAY-ALONG

 Audio Access Included

Visit **www.halleonard.com/mylibrary**

Enter Code
1869-9751-7665-2481

CLASSICAL THEMES
FOR ALTO SAX

T0080166

CONTENTS

Audio Arrangements by Peter Deneff
Tracking, mixing, and mastering by BeatHouse Music

ISBN 978-1-4803-6049-5

7777 W. BLUEMOUND RD. P.O. BOX 13819 MILWAUKEE, WI 53213

In Australia Contact:
Hal Leonard Australia Pty. Ltd.
4 Lentara Court
Cheltenham, Victoria, 3192 Australia
Email: ausadmin@halleonard.com.au

Visit Hal Leonard Online at
www.halleonard.com

FINLANDIA

By JEAN SIBELIUS

MORNING
from PEER GYNT

By EDVARD GRIEG

SYMPHONY NO. 1
Fourth Movement Excerpt

By JOHANNES BRAHMS

CARNIVAL OF VENICE

By JULIUS BENEDICT

SPRING
from THE FOUR SEASONS

By ANTONIO VIVALDI

CAN CAN
from ORPHEUS IN THE UNDERWORLD

By JACQUES OFFENBACH

Briskly, with energy

MUSETTE
from THE ANNA MAGDALENA NOTEBOOK

By JOHANN SEBASTIAN BACH

Moderately

TRUMPET VOLUNTARY
(Prince of Denmark's March)

By JEREMIAH CLARKE

LARGO

from SYMPHONY NO. 9 ("New World")

By ANTONIN DVOŘÁK

Slowly, with feeling

ODE TO JOY

from SYMPHONY NO. 9

By LUDWIG VAN BEETHOVEN

Moderately